Living in the
1980s

Rosemary Rees & Judith Maguire

Heinemann

Heinemann Library,
an imprint of Heinemann Publishers (Oxford) Ltd,
Halley Court, Jordan Hill, Oxford, OX2 8EJ

OXFORD LONDON EDINBURGH
MADRID PARIS ATHENS BOLOGNA
MELBOURNE SYDNEY AUCKLAND
SINGAPORE TOKYO IBADAN
NAIROBI GABORONE HARARE
PORTSMOUTH NH (USA)

First published 1993
93 94 95 96 10 9 8 7 6 5 4 3 2 1

British Library Cataloguing in Publication Data
is available on request from the British Library.

ISBN 0 431 07214 0

Designed by Philip Parkhouse
Printed and bound in China

Acknowledgements
The authors and publisher would like to thank the following
for permission to reproduce photographs:
Collections/David Bowie: p. 15
Collections/Brian Shuel: p. 14
Collections/Anthea Sieveking: p. 11
Edifice/Lewis: p. 27
Eye Ubiquitous/Paul Prestidge: p. 22
Eye Ubiquitous/Ben Spencer: p. 24
Impact/Peter Arkell: p.10, /Lionel Derimais: p. 7, /John Evens: p. 20,
/Jeremy Nicholl: p. 30, /Caroline Penn: p. 23, /Geray Sweeney: p. 17
National Trust Photographic Library: p. 26
Philip Parkhouse: p.21, /Rex Features: pp. 4, 28
Sally and Richard Greenhill: pp. 5, 6, 8, 9, 13, 19, 25
Science Photo Library/Martin Dohrn: p. 18
Science Photo Library/John Heseltine: p. 16

Cover photograph: Ace Photo Agency/Gabe Palmer

Contents

Home 1

These houses were built in the 1980s.
They were made to look like old houses.
They had wooden windows and doors.
They had front gardens with
no walls or fences.
Some had different windows.
Some had different roofs.
When was your house built?

This kitchen had lots of things in it,
to make cooking easier.
There was a microwave oven, a toaster
and an electric kettle.
There was a dishwasher to make
washing-up faster and easier.

Home 2

In the 1980s, nearly all families had televisions.

Some families had big televisions, and some had small ones like this.

People had lots more machines in their homes.

They had video recorders and tape recorders. Some had compact disc players.

Big supermarkets like this one were built outside towns.

This was so people had plenty of space to park their cars.

There was lots of different food to choose from in the supermarkets.

Some of the food was kept fresh by freezing it.

Home 3

Big cities often had shopping centres.
When it rained, people could go from
shop to shop without getting wet.
In most shopping centres there was
somewhere you could eat.
Some shopping centres had areas for
children to play in.

These people had a barbecue in
their garden.
The man cooked the food on the fire.
He had to try hard not to burn it.
Some people had barbecue parties with
their friends.
Everyone brought their own food and
cooked it on the fire.

School 1

These children used the school computer.
It helped them with their work.
Children really liked working and playing
on the computer.
Children learnt how to use computers very
quickly. Sometimes they learnt faster than
their teachers.

These children did a play in school about the Romans.
The children had to make their costumes.
They worked hard to learn their words.
They showed the play to the other children and the mums and dads.
Everyone thought it was very good.

School 2

These children had a sports day
at school.
They had races against each other.
Some schools practised a lot before
the sports day.
The mums and dads, who came to
watch, had their own races too.

These children made models in school.
The girls made a model of a big ship.
The children learnt how to use the
computers to make things move.
They used the computers to make their
models move.

Work 1

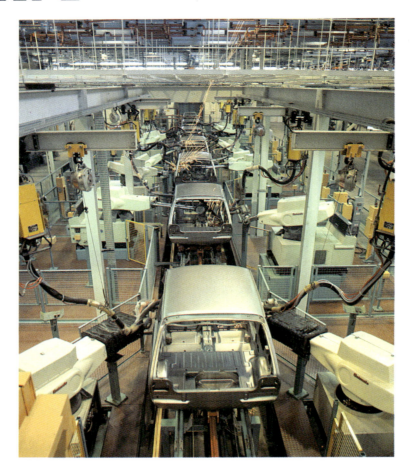

These machines built cars.
People were not needed to build the cars.
Just a few people were needed to look after the machines.
Lots of people did not have jobs.
The machines did the jobs that the people used to do.

This machine was used to cut corn.
The farmer liked using the machine.
It was fast and cost less money than
using people to cut the corn.
He could cut the corn in lots of fields in
one day.

Work 2

This farmer did not have a big machine to collect his corn.
He had to collect it by tractor.
He had to use a big fork to throw the corn on top of the tractor.
He had to be very strong.
It took a long time to collect the corn.

These people worked in a big office.
Most people in the office used computers.
Computers were used to send messages.
Computers made sending messages faster.
People were able to work better and faster
with computers.

Spare Time 1

This boy played on his computer game.
People bought computers to use at home.
There were computers to do work on, and
to play games on.
Lots of the computers plugged into
the television.

These people did a keep fit class.
Lots of people tried to get fitter.
They were more careful about the food
they ate.
Some people went jogging.
How do you keep fit?

Spare Time 2

This girl rode her BMX bike.
She was very good at it.
She did some very good stunts.
She had to work hard to be this good.
Lots of children had BMX bikes.
Some of them went to parks to learn to ride them well.

This family watched a video in their living room.

Lots of families had video recorders.

They watched films at home instead of going to the cinema.

People could record programmes they liked and watch them when they wanted.

Spare Time 3

These people are windsurfing.
When the wind blows, they go across the water very fast.
It is hard to stay on the board.
When they were learning to windsurf, they fell in the water a lot.
People tried many new sports in the 1980s.

These children were at an after-school
club.
The girls played snooker.
Lots of schools had after-school clubs or
youth clubs.
Children could play lots of different games
there.
There were tuck-shops that sold sweets
and drinks.

Holidays 1

This girl was a student in the 1980s.
For her holidays, she travelled to lots of places by train.
With only one ticket, she could go on lots of different trains.
It was a cheap way to travel.
Lots of young people went on holiday like this.

This was a park were people went to find out about the past.

People were dressed up in different clothes.

They showed how food was cooked in the olden days.

People spent the day here.

Some people went for days out, instead of going on holiday.

Holidays 2

These people spent their holiday time mending these broken walls.

They did not get paid.

There were lots of holidays, where people worked for free.

In the 1980s people worried about the earth and how they looked after it.

These people spent their holiday
at Disneyland.
Lots of big fun-parks were built in
the 1980s.
They had lots of fast and scary rides.
Children and grown-ups really liked them.
It cost a lot of money to go into the park,
but you did not pay to go on the rides.

Special Days 1

These children played on a bouncy castle.
They had to take their shoes off so that
they did not get hurt.
The bouncy castle was at a summer fair.
The children had to pay money to go
on the bouncy castle.
This money was used to help other people.

In July 1985, there was a big concert in London. The concert was called Live Aid. Lots of famous people sang at the concert. People paid a lot of money to see them sing.
The money was used to help the starving people in Africa.

Special Days 2

This little girl had her birthday party at a Wimpy Bar.

The children had burgers and chips to eat. They had milkshakes to drink.

The girl had a big birthday cake.

The children were given special hats to wear.

They were given little toys to take home.

Time Line

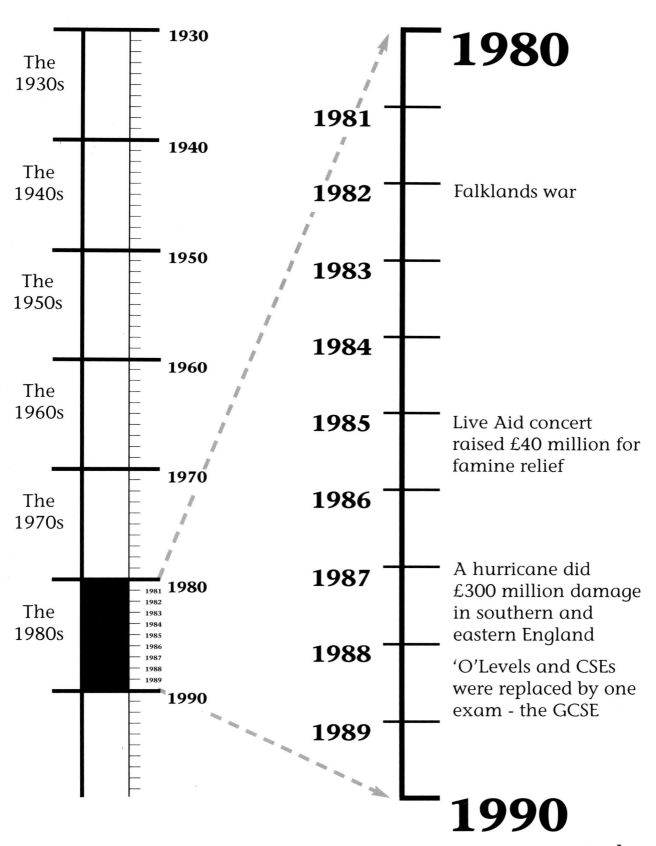

The 1930s

The 1940s

The 1950s

The 1960s

The 1970s

The 1980s

1930
1940
1950
1960
1970
1980
1990

1981
1982
1983
1984
1985
1986
1987
1988
1989

1980

1981

1982   Falklands war

1983

1984

1985   Live Aid concert raised £40 million for famine relief

1986

1987   A hurricane did £300 million damage in southern and eastern England

1988   'O'Levels and CSEs were replaced by one exam - the GCSE

1989

1990

Index